EROTIC ART PHOTOGRAPHY

VOL. 5

MORE
COUPLES
1890 – 1930

JANSSEN

© 2001 JANSSEN PUBLISHERS CC

P.O.BOX 404, SIMONS' TOWN, 7995, SOUTH AFRICA

PRODUCTION: DRUCK- UND VERLAGSHAUS ERFURT GMBH

PRINTED IN GERMANY

DISTRIBUTION: LKG, PÖTZSCHAUER WEG,   D-04579 ESPENHAIN, GERMANY

DISTRIBUTION USA: BOOKAZINE CO.INC., 75, HOOK RD., BAYONNE, N.Y.07002

ISBN: 0-9584314-7 -7

NOT FOR SALE TO MINORS UNDER 18 YEARS

EMAIL PUBLISHERS OFFICE: JANSSENP@IAFRICA.COM

PLEASE VISIT OUR WEBSITE UNDER: **WWW.JANSSENBOOKS.CO.ZA**

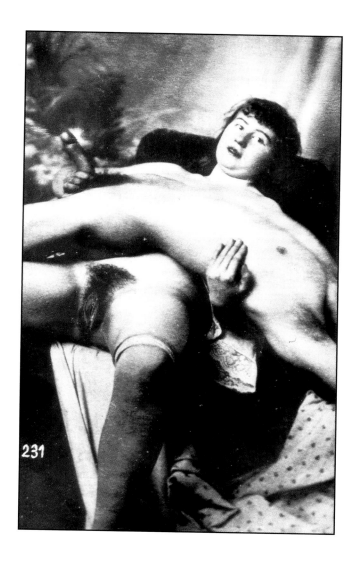

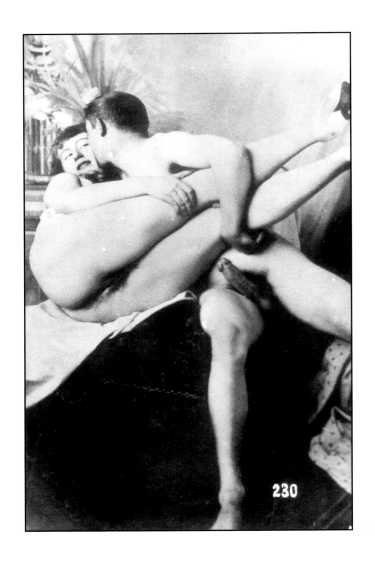

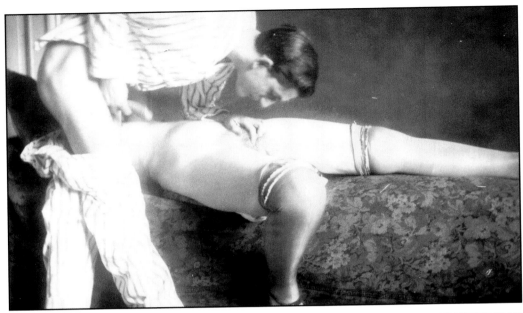

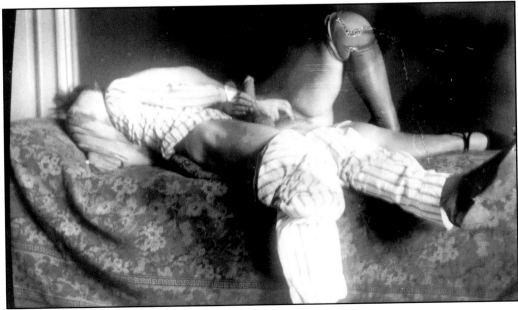

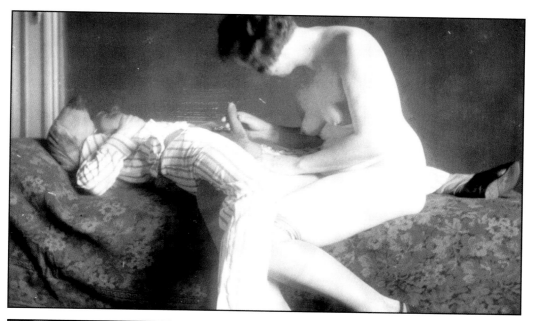

15

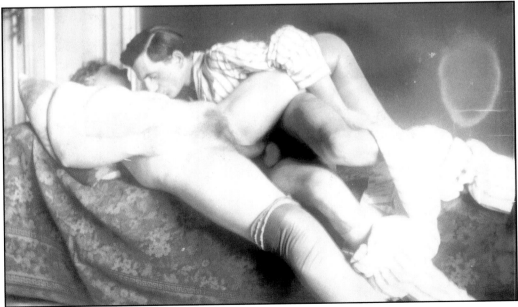

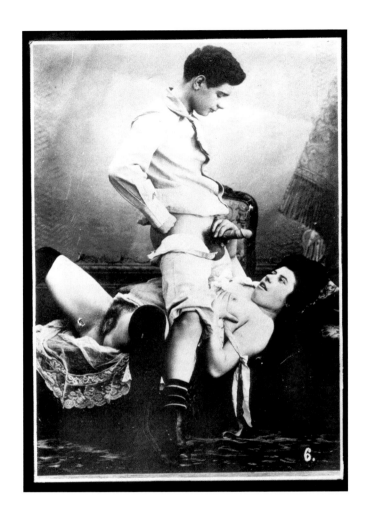

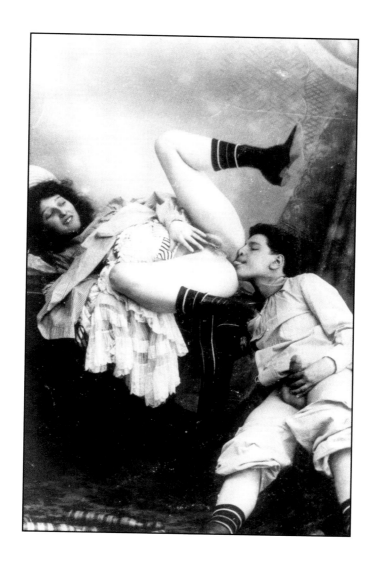

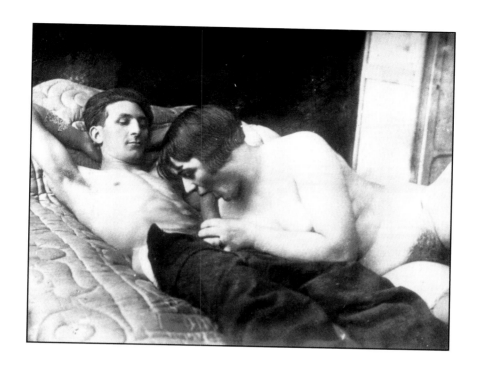

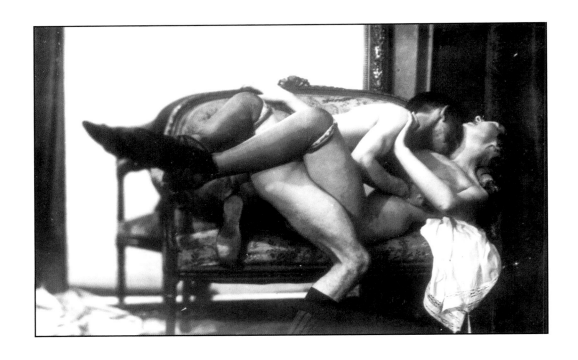

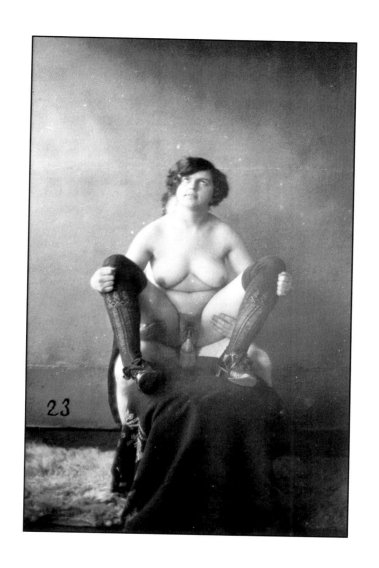

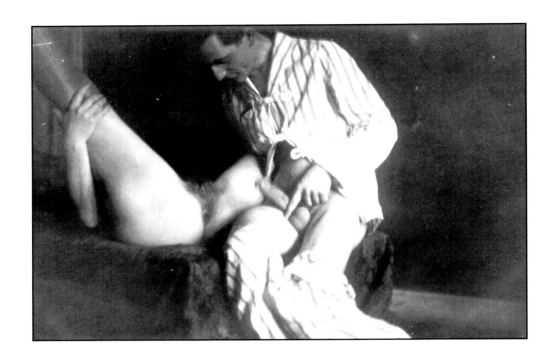

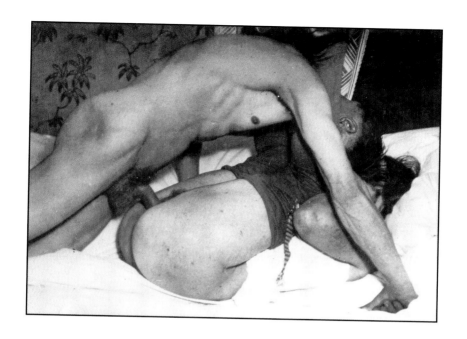

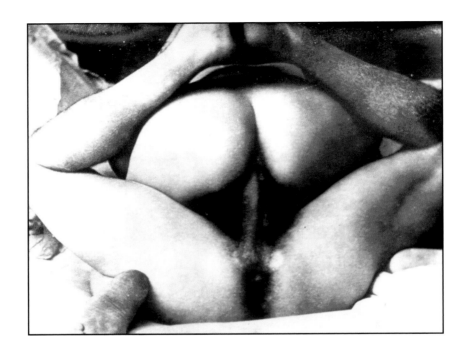

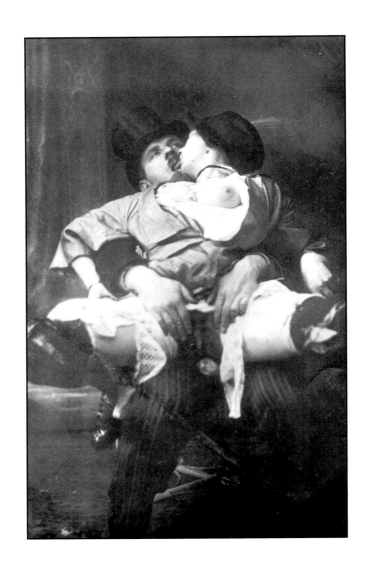

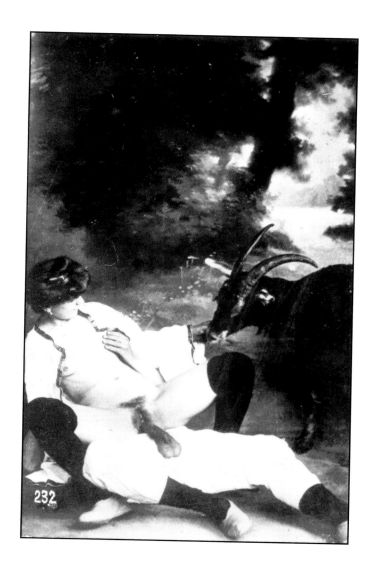

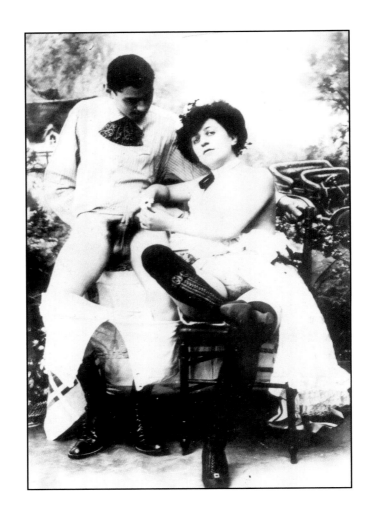

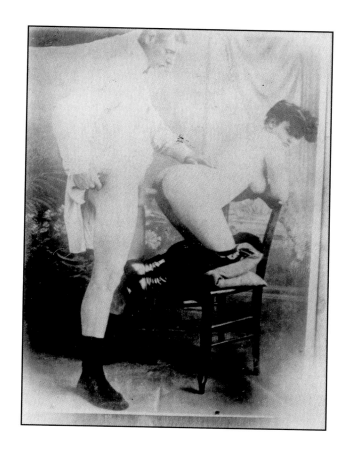

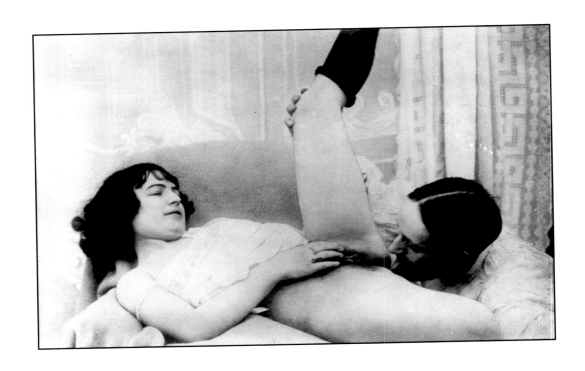

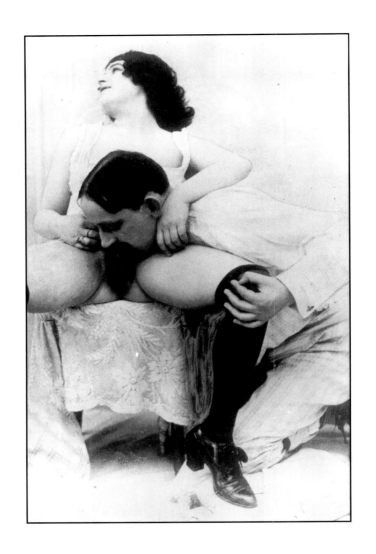

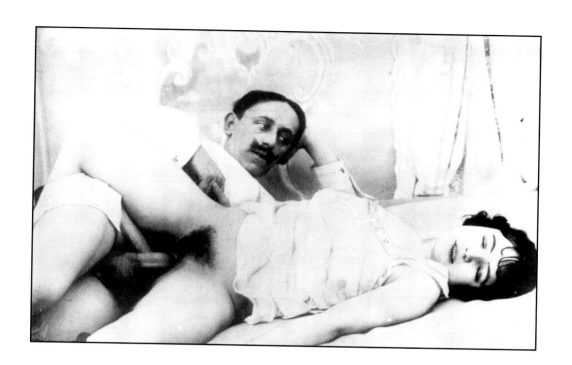

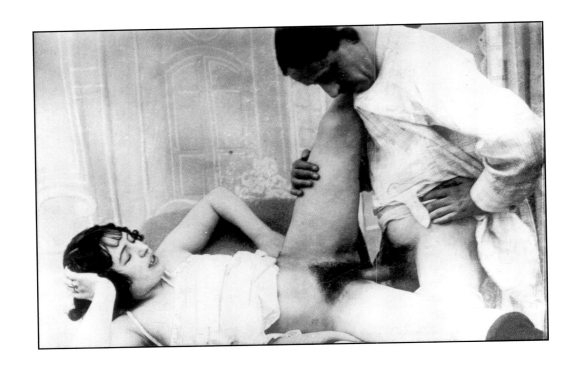

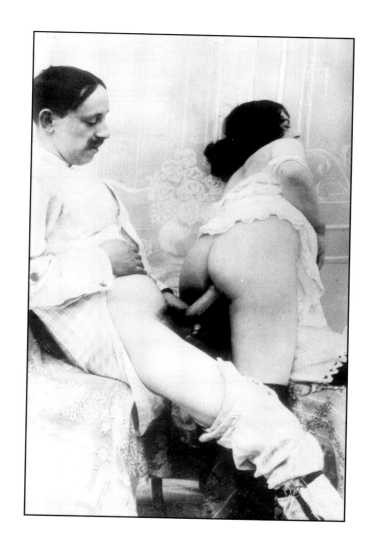

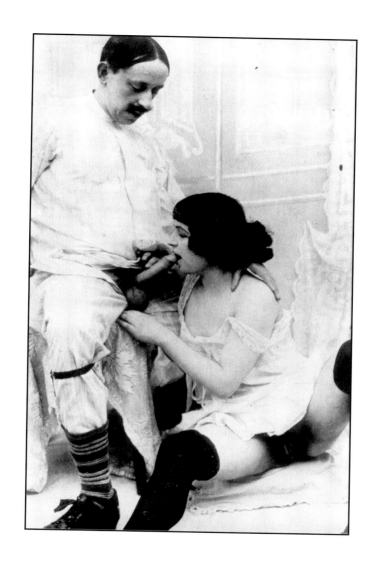

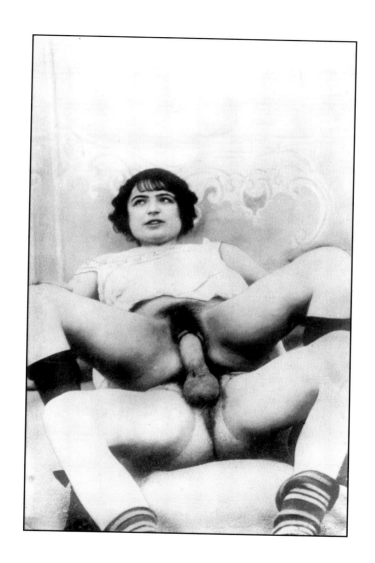

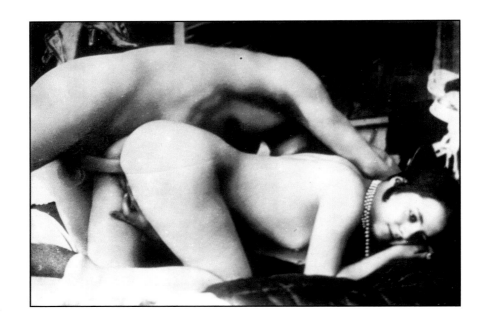

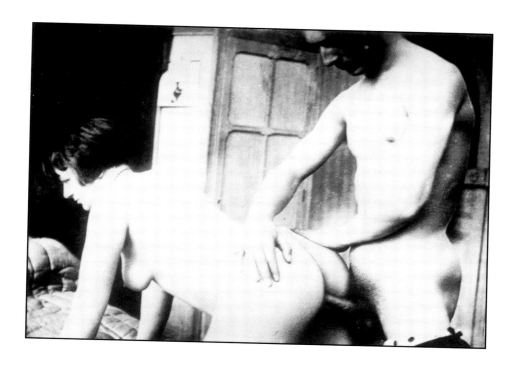

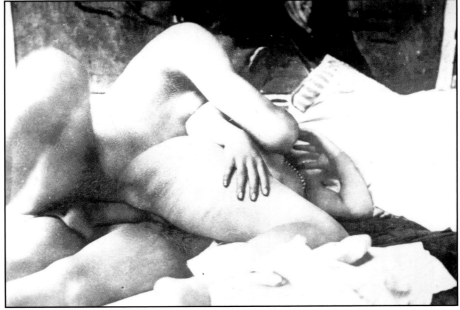

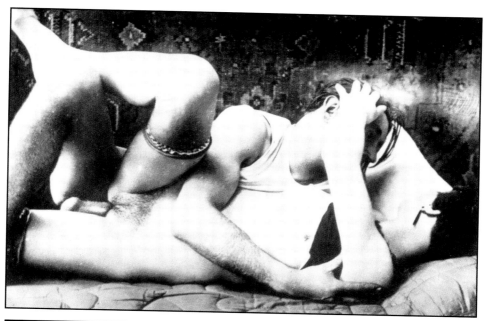

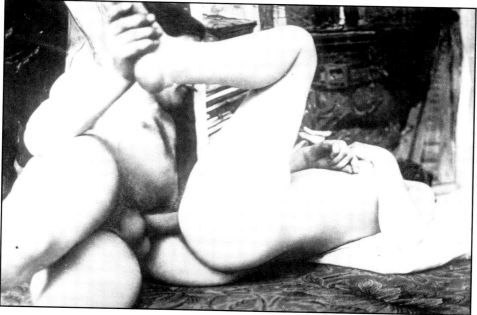